John W. Garrett

American Numismatic Society Correspondence

1920 - 1923

John W. Garrett

American Numismatic Society Correspondence
1920 - 1923

ISBN/EAN: 9783743328228

Manufactured in Europe, USA, Canada, Australia, Japa

Cover: Foto ©Andreas Hilbeck / pixelio.de

Manufactured and distributed by brebook publishing software (www.brebook.com)

John W. Garrett

American Numismatic Society Correspondence

New York, January 6, 1920

Hon. John W. Garrett
    Care Robert Garrett & Sons
        Garrett Building
            Baltimore, Md.

To The American Numismatic Society, Dr.

BROADWAY, BETWEEN 155TH AND 156TH STREETS

Associate Membership Dues for 19 20 $5.00

Received Payment,

Treasurer.

Membership Medal (Silver, $8.00; Bronze, $4.00), may be obtained from the Treasurer.

(See other side)

THE AMERICAN NUMISMATIC SOCIETY
BROADWAY, BETWEEN 155TH
AND 156TH STREETS
NEW YORK

January 6, 1920

Dr. Henry Barton Jacobs
11 Mt. Vernon Place, West
Baltimore, Maryland

Dear Sir:

I beg to acknowledge receipt of your letter of the
2nd enclosing cheque for your annual dues. Thank you very much.

Thank you also for your proposal for membership
of the Hon. John W. Garrett, American Minister to the Hague.
At a meeting of the Council yesterday, his name was presented,
and he was unanimously elected. Please assure Mr. Garrett that
that we shall be very glad to welcome him at our Museum whenever
he may be in New York. I trust we may have the pleasure of
greeting you here too should opportunity serve you when you are
in this city.

Very respectfully yours,

Sydney P. Noe

Secretary.

THE AMERICAN NUMISMATIC SOCIETY
BROADWAY. BETWEEN 155TH
AND 156TH STREETS
NEW YORK

January 6, 1920

Hon. John W. Garrett
      Care Robert Garrett & Sons
            Garrett Building
                Baltimore, Md..

Dear Sir:

      I have the honor to inform you that at ~~the last~~ yesterday's
meeting of the Council you were unanimously elected an Associate of The American Numismatic Society, upon the nomination
of Sydney P. Noe.

      It gave us great pleasure to receive Dr. Jacobs'
proposal of your name for membership, and if when you have an
opportunity for visiting our Museum you will make yourself
known, I should be very glad to show any of our material not on
exhibition which might be of interest to you.

        Very respectfully yours,

        Sydney P. Noe

           Secretary.

THE AMERICAN NUMISMATIC SOCIETY
BROADWAY, BETWEEN 155TH
AND 156TH STREETS
NEW YORK

January 20th 1920.

Mr John W. Garrett,
3 Stockton Street, Princeton, N. J.

My dear Mr Garrett:—

Mr Wood and I have been trying to get away this week, but find it impossible. Next week, if you are still in Princeton, we could spend Tuesday there, or Friday. We will hold these dates — 2nd ... 30th until we hear from you. I hope we can get together and be of use to you.

Very sincerely

John Frien Jr.

after luncheon.

THE AMERICAN NUMISMATIC SOCIETY
BROADWAY, BETWEEN 155TH
AND 156TH STREETS
NEW YORK

February 13, 1920

John W. Garrett, Esq.
     C/o Robert Garrett & Sons
          Garrett Building
               Baltimore, Md.

My dear Mr. Garrett:

I wish to thank you most sincerely for the kind
hospitality shown me on my recent trip to Princeton. This I
enjoyed very much, and I do not hesitate to say that I hope
to view the collection again some time after my return from
Europe.

I trust to see you up here before very long.

We have all the Journals that you want, and some
of the Proceedings. These I am sending you by express to 3⁻
Stockton Street, Princeton.

I beg to remain,

Very truly,

Howland Wood
                              Curator.

John W. Garrett, Esq.
3 Stockton Street
Princeton, N.J.

To The American Numismatic Society, Dr.

BROADWAY, BETWEEN 155TH AND 156TH STREETS

American Journal of Numismatics, Vols. 18, 23-42 inc., @ $2.00 .... $42.00
" " " " Vol. 43 (Nos. 1-3) 1.50
" " " " Vols. 48, 49, 50, @ $5 . . . . . . 15.00
Proceedings and Papers 1888-1919 inc. No charge
                                                    $58.50

Received payment,

Arthur C. Hoyman
— or Treasurer.

Dear Mr. Wood:

I am very much obliged to you for your letter
of February 13th and for the trouble you have taken to get me
the copies of the Journal and some of the proceedings that I
need.   I was at Princeton yesterday and they had not yet
arrived there. If they have not been sent, I suggest that
you hold them and I will call for them at the earliest possible opportunity.   I am obliged to be out of town for
three or four days but I may be able to come up to the Museum
on Saturday next.

I greatly enjoyed your visit to Princeton
and hope that you will come again.

Sincerely yours,

Howland Wood, Esquire,
Curator, The American Numismatic Society,
Broadway, bet. 155th and 156th Sts.,
New York.

May 24th, 1920.

Dear Mr. Wood:

While I was Minister to The Argentine, I took considerable interest - among other things + in the schools, one result of which was that I was presented, I think by the Minister for Education, with a number of medals commemorating the founding of various schools in the nation. I have had them packed away for several years and came across them the other day, and I wondered whether they would be acceptable to the Society. I shall send them to you by express in the hope that you will care to have them.

a good deal of eagerness the Miller sale. I am sorry that I am not collecting Roman coins, for I should like to get some of the wonderful things that are being disposed of by Mr. Elder. There are a few Colonial pieces that I am putting in bids on, but there are not many that I really want for my collection.

I hope to be in New York next month and have the pleasure of seeing you again.

Very sincerely yours,

Howland Wood, Esq.,
Curator,
The Am.Numismatic Society,
Broadway, bet.155th & 156th Sts.,
NEW YORK CITY.

OFFICE OF
THE SECRETARY

TELEPHONE
AUDUBON 2484

THE
AMERICAN
NUMISMATIC
SOCIETY

PARVA
NE
PEREANT

MUSEUM OPEN
10 · 5, WEEK-DAYS
1 · 5, SUNDAYS

LIBRARY OPEN
10 · 5, WEEK-DAYS

THE AMERICAN NUMISMATIC SOCIETY
BROADWAY, BETWEEN 155TH
AND 156TH STREETS
NEW YORK

May 28th, 1920

Hon. John W. Garrett
Evergreen-on-Avenue
Baltimore, Md.

My dear Mr. Garrett:

As Mr. Wood has gone to Europe, your letter to him
came to me. It was very thoughtful of you to remember us
in connection with the Argentine medals and we shall be glad
to add them to our Collection. It is just such medals as
these that are always so difficult to acquire, and yet for
the purpose of making our Cabinet complete we really should
have them.

Very truly yours,

Arthur C. Wyman

Assistant to Curator

W/E

JOHN REILLY, JR.
169 EAST 71ST STREET
NEW YORK CITY

Amagansett, L.I., N.Y.
August 19th 1928

Dear Mr Garrett:

Yours of July 31st awaited my return last night. Sorry not to give you quicker action. However, I will send your list of Journals wanted to Mr Noe our secretary, at the Society. He will promptly mail them to you at Port Chester.

Mr Wood is expected from England after the middle of September.

I expect to remain in Amagansett until the end of next month.

Trusting you are enjoying your summer, I am,

Very sincerely -

John Reilly Jr.

New York, August 23rd, 1920.

Mr. John Garrett,
   Meade House, Quaker Ridge,
      Port Chester, N. Y.

To The American Numismatic Society, Dr.

BROADWAY, BETWEEN 155TH AND 156TH STREETS

American Journal of Numismatics:

Vol. XXII,	No. 4,	$ .50	
" XLIII,	" 4,	.50	
" XLIV,	" 3 & 4,	1.00	
" XLV,	" 3 & 4,	1.00	
" XLVI,	" 1 - 4,	2.00	
" LII,		5.00	$10.00

Received payment,

American Numismatic

           Treasurer.

THE AMERICAN NUMISMATIC SOCIETY
BROADWAY, BETWEEN 155TH
AND 156TH STREETS
NEW YORK

August 24th, 1920.

John Garrett, Esq.,
    Meade House, Quaker Ridge,
        Port Chester, N. Y.

Dear Sir:-

        At the request of Mr. John Reilly, Jr., I am
sending you the Journals called for on the accompanying
memorandum. I took the liberty of omitting one or two
which I found duplicated in the lot sent you earlier
in the year. If for any reason you desire additional
copies, or have parted with those sent you at that time,
please let me know and I will send immediately whatever
you may still like.

                    Very respectfully yours,

                    Sydney R Noe
                            Secretary.

Sent check for 10.00
asked for 4 numbers
still needed :

OFFICE OF
THE SECRETARY

TELEPHONE
AUDUBON 2484

CABLE ADDRESS
"NUMISMA" NEW YORK

MUSEUM OPEN
10 - 5. WEEK-DAYS
1 - 5. SUNDAYS

LIBRARY OPEN
10 - 5. WEEK-DAYS

THE AMERICAN NUMISMATIC SOCIETY
BROADWAY, BETWEEN 155TH
AND 156TH STREETS
NEW YORK

August 31st, 1920.

Mr. John W. Garrett,
    Meade House, Quaker Ridge,
      Port Chester, N. Y.

Dear Mr. Garrett:-

    I have your letter of the 27th, and we are sending
you today the lacking numbers of the Journal. The numbers of Volume XLIII should have been sent with the first
lot for which you have already paid, and number one of
Volume XLV is covered by one of the parts returned. For
the other two parts you are therefore entitled to a
credit of one dollar which I am enclosing.

               Very respectfully yours,

                          Secretary.

THE AMERICAN NUMISMATIC SOCIETY
BROADWAY, BETWEEN 155TH
AND 156TH STREETS
NEW YORK

December 10th, 1920.

Hon. John W. Garrett,
3 Stockton St.,
Princeton, N. J.

Dear Sir:-

At a recent meeting of the Council of The
American Numismatic Society, it was decided to publish
the proceedings and reports of our meetings in brochure
form in the series of Numismatic Notes and Monographs,
beginning January 1921.

Under an arrangement with the publishers of
The Numismatist, this periodical has been sent to you
heretofore at our expense in order that information regarding meetings of our Society might reach you. The
cost of doing this has come from our general funds which
are limited. Recently, there has come the opportunity
for publishing our proceedings in the new form. As they
will be sent to all our members, there is not the same
need for continuing our arrangements with the Numismatist,
and after January 1921 you will no longer receive copies
of this magazine by reason of your membership in our
Society.

Our relations with the editors and publishers
of the Numismatist continue to be of the friendliest.
If you have found in the Numismatist interesting and
valuable reading matter, we trust that you will respond
favorably to the accompanying invitation of the editor
of this magazine by becoming a regular subscriber.

Very respectfully yours,

Secretary.

OFFICE OF
THE CURATOR

TELEPHONE
AUDUBON 2484

CABLE ADDRESS
"NUMISMA" NEW YORK

MUSEUM OPEN
10 · 5, WEEK-DAYS
1 · 5, SUNDAYS

LIBRARY OPEN
10 · 5, WEEK-DAYS

THE AMERICAN NUMISMATIC SOCIETY
BROADWAY, BETWEEN 155TH
AND 156TH STREETS
NEW YORK

Decc ber 18th, 1920

John W. Garrett, Esq.
Garrett Building
Baltimore, Md.

My dear Mr. Garrett:

We were successful in getting most of the
Indian Peace Medals which we wanted in Mr. Chap-
man's recent sale. We got the two we most desired, namely, the American Fur Company medal
with the head of John Jacob Astor on it, and the
large size Jefferson medal as well as several of
the minor Colonial ones. These cost us $698.00.
We would have gotten more if we had felt that we
had more money to spend.

We would appreciate it very much if you would
send us a cheque by the first of the year. I
think Miss Reilly told me that you had said you
would subscribe Fifty Dollars; I want to thank you
most sincerely for this.

I understand that you are now much interested
in Greek coins. As you may know, we have some
very fine ones here, and Mr. Newell has one of the
finest collections in the world. He would be very
pleased to show you his pieces if at any time you
would let us know when you could come up so that I
could arrange a time which would also be convenient
to Mr. Newell.

Very truly yours,

Curator

HW/E

Mr. John W. Garrett,
  c/o Robert Garrett & Sons,
     Garrett Building,
        Baltimore, Md.

ᴛᴏ The American Numismatic Society. ᴅʀ.

BROADWAY, BETWEEN 155TH AND 156TH STREETS

————————➤◄————————

Associate Membership Dues for 19 31 $5.00

Received Payment,

                                                              Treasurer.

Membership Medal (Silver, $8.00; Bronze, $4.00), may be obtained from the Treasurer.

(See other side)

Any Member or Associate Member in arrears for more than one year shall be dropped from the roll after due notification. But may be reinstated by resolution of the Council upon payment of the arrears.

OFFICE OF
THE CURATOR

TELEPHONE
AUDUBON 2484

MUSEUM OPEN
10 - 5, WEEK-DAYS
1 - 5, SUNDAYS

LIBRARY OPEN
10 - 5, WEEK-DAYS

THE AMERICAN NUMISMATIC SOCIETY
BROADWAY, BETWEEN 155TH
AND 156TH STREETS
NEW YORK

January 5th, 1911

John W. Garrett, Esq,
55 West 57, New York

My dear Mr. Garrett:

Please accept my apologies for not acknowledging your donation of Fifty Dollars (\$50.00) before this. I beg to thank you very much indeed for this cheque.

I have been hoping that you would get up here with the coins which you want to attribute; we can accommodate you in good shape, and trust that you will be up here soon.

Very truly yours,

Howland Wood

Curator

HW./s

THE AMERICAN RED CROSS MEDAL.

Designed by DANIEL C. FRENCH

AMERICAN RED CROSS

THE AMERICAN NUMISMATIC SOCIETY

THE WAR COUNCIL MEDAL

New York, January 15th, 1921

The American Red Cross on the occasion of its annual meeting of the present year presented to each member of its War Council a memorial medal in recognition of their exceptional services during the war. This medal has been designed by Daniel C. French and executed under his direction.

The twelve medals given to the members of the War Council were struck in gold. Each bears on its rim the name of its recipient. Each is, therefore, unique and is intended so to be. In addition four copies in silver have been issued.

The interest in this medal is so great and its beauty so exceptional that the committee in charge, with the approval of the National Society, have determined to give to Chapters and members of the Red Cross as well as to art museums and lovers of art the opportunity of securing a limited number of replicas in bronze. The half tone reproduction on the preceding page will give an idea of the beauty and dignity of Mr. French's achievement. On the obverse, in high relief, is represented the symbolic head of an American soldier. Mr. French's initials, D C. F., will be found inconspicuously beneath the neck of the figure. On the reverse is a Red Cross nurse standing erect over a prostrate wounded soldier. The two figures are posed in the form of a cross and are appropriately enclosed in the typical form of an American Red Cross. On the reverse is the following inscription: AMERICAN RED CROSS. TO COMMEMORATE THE VISION AND ACHIEVEMENT OF ITS WAR COUNCIL. The diameter of the medal is 2¾ inches.

The subscription price of the bronze medal has been fixed at $6.00, an amount deemed sufficient substantially to cover cost of the materials and distribution. All the medals will be numbered. The allotment and numbering of the medals will be made in the order of receipt of subscriptions. The lists will close at noon on March 15 1921, after which date no more subscriptions will be accepted. Subscriptions must be accompanied by check to the order of the American Numismatic Society and instructions for delivery should be sent, *not* to the Red Cross or the Red Cross Committee, but to THE AMERICAN NUMISMATIC SOCIETY, 156TH ST. and BROADWAY, NEW YORK, who have kindly consented to make this distribution.

Robert W. de Forest
Livingston Farrand
John M. Glenn
War Council Medal Committee
of The American Red Cross

Edward T. Newell
John Reilly, Jr.
Archer M. Huntington
William B. Osgood Field
Henry Russell Drowne
of The American Numismatic Society

Hon. John W. Garrett,
  c/o Robert Garrett & Sons,
    Garrett Building,
      Baltimore, Maryland.

To The American Numismatic Society, Dr.

BROADWAY, BETWEEN 155TH AND 156TH STREETS

————————— ✄ —————————

Membership Dues for 1921, · · · · · · ·	$15.00
Associate Membership Dues for 1921 paid January 8th, 1921. ·	5.00
	$10.00

Received Payment,

John Reilly Treasurer.

Membership Medal (Silver, $8.00; Bronze, $4.00), may be obtained from the Treasurer.

(See other side)

OFFICE OF
THE SECRETARY

TELEPHONE
AUDUBON 2484

CABLE ADDRESS
"NUMISMA" NEW YORK

MUSEUM OPEN
10 - 5, WEEK-DAYS
1 - 5, SUNDAYS

LIBRARY OPEN
10 - 5, WEEK-DAYS

THE AMERICAN NUMISMATIC SOCIETY
BROADWAY, BETWEEN 155TH
AND 156TH STREETS
NEW YORK

January 15th, 1921.

Hon. John W. Garrett,
    c/o Robert Garrett & Sons,
        Garrett Building,
            Baltimore, Md.

Dear Mr. Garrett:-

    It gives me great pleasure to inform you that
at the meeting of the Council held yesterday, you
were unanimously elected a Fellow of The American
Numismatic Society.

                    Very respectfully yours,

                    Sydney P. Noe

                            Secretary.

OFFICE OF
THE TREASURER

TELEPHONE
AUDUBON 2484

MUSEUM OPEN
10 · 5. WEEK-DAYS
1 · 5. SUNDAYS
LIBRARY OPEN
10 · 5. WEEK-DAYS

THE AMERICAN NUMISMATIC SOCIETY
BROADWAY, BETWEEN 155TH
AND 156TH STREETS
NEW YORK

March 2nd, 1921

John W. Garrett, Esq.
The Garrett Building
Baltimore, Md.

Dear Sir:

Through a recently communicated ruling of
the Collector of Internal Revenue, contributions
made by individuals to this Society are deductible
in reporting on their incomes for the Income Tax.
This circumstance is communicated to you in order
that you may so record your much appreciated contribution during the year 1920.

Very cordially yours,

John Reilly

Treasurer

THE AMERICAN NUMISMATIC SOCIETY
BROADWAY, BETWEEN 155TH
AND 156TH STREETS
NEW YORK

May 2nd, 1921.

Mr. John W. Garrett,
     Garrett Building,
          Baltimore, Md.

Dear Mr. Garrett:-

     I understand that you have one of the large oval
Indian peace medals of Washington which is different
from any in this Society's collection.

     We would greatly appreciate it if you would be
willing to place this on loan here for awhile thereby
giving us the opportunity of studying it and comparing
it with those that we have.

     My impression is that your medal is of a little
later type than the large one we have, and probably by
a different engraver.

     While each individual medal of this series was en-
graved by hand and consequently will vary in some par-
ticulars from others, there are, as far as I can make
out four distinct varieties of which we have three and
yours is the fourth.

     The first variety bears one date only - 1789.
The second and third each have two dates - 1792 and 1793.
The difference being large and small size, and the fourth
variety has the dates 1793 and 1795.

     Hoping you will consider this favorably, and with
kind regards, I am,

                         Very truly yours,

                         Chairman, Committee on Indian Medals.

OFFICE OF
THE CURATOR

TELEPHONE
AUDUBON 2484

CABLE ADDRESS
"NUMISMA" NEW YORK

MUSEUM OPEN
10 - 5, WEEK-DAYS
1 - 5, SUNDAYS

LIBRARY OPEN
10 - 5, WEEK-DAYS

THE AMERICAN NUMISMATIC SOCIETY
BROADWAY, BETWEEN 155TH
AND 156TH STREETS
NEW YORK

May 13th, 1921

John W. Garrett, Esq.
Garrett Building
Baltimore, Md.

Dear Mr. Garrett:

I received from Mr. Wayte Raymond
the other day the Indian Peace Medal as
well as the Lord Baltimore medal which
you so kindly turned over to me on loan,
and of which we will take the best of
care until you call for them.

Very truly yours,

Howland Wood
Curator

HW/E

Mrs. Bowman B. Selden, Chairman,
Committee on Indian Medals,
American Numismatics Society,
Broadway & 156th Street, New York, N. Y.

Dear Mr. Selden -

      I took the Washington medal, about
which you wrote me in your letter of April 2nd, with me
to New York a few days ago and gave it to Mr. Wayte Raymond,
who was kind enough to say that he would leave it for me at
the Numismatic Society. I hope you will see that it is well
taken care of, and I shall be very much interested in knowing the result of your inquiries.

                Yours very truly,

                        John W. Garrett.

May 25th, 1921.

Mr. John W. Garrett,
Garrett Building,
Baltimore, Md.

Dear Mr. Garrett:-

I had the pleasure of looking at your Washington medal a few days ago, and it confirms my opinion that these oval Washington medals are by three different engravers, showing three styles of work.

The one of 1789, of which we have the only specimen that I have seen or heard of, is very crude and quite different from the others.

Then came the two sizes of 1792 and 1793 all of which are quite similar and evidently by the same hand. We have the large one of 1793 and the small one of 1792.

Lastly those of 1793 and 1795, with the initials J. R. (Joseph Richardson of Philadelphia), and which differ in several ways from the others.

I am very glad to have the chance of comparing your medal of 1795 with those in the Society's collection, and hope that you will not be in a hurry to take your medal away as it is of great interest and advantage to have the different varities where they can all be seen and studied at the same time.

Taken with
I = 1/25? 29 Xi

his left hand and a wine cup (canthamus) in his right hand. These are attributes only of Dionysos or Bacchus. The animals are certainly of Apollo(?) leopards and not lions which is again only suitable for Bacchus.

Your coin is indeed a gem, and you are to be congratulated in having

exactly that of Caracalla before he commenced to raise a beard. The number of the Tribunician Power is that of Caracalla - but not of Elagabalus.

The reverse design is certainly that of Dionysos in a quadriga of leopards. Teino is shown by the fact that the glory has a Telegram in

My dear Dr. de Youanna

Since I have returned
to the city I have had more
opportunities to study the
photographs of the beautiful
armour you purchased a little
while ago. I am more
convinced that if we should

With best wishes and hoping
you are daily adding fine
pieces to your splendid collection

Sincerely

Edward T. Newell

OFFICE OF
THE CURATOR

TELEPHONE
AUDUBON 2484

CABLE ADDRESS
NUMISMA" NEW YORK

MUSEUM OPEN
10 - 5, WEEK-DAYS
1 - 5, SUNDAYS

LIBRARY OPEN
10 - 5, WEEK-DAYS

THE AMERICAN NUMISMATIC SOCIETY
BROADWAY, BETWEEN 155TH
AND 156TH STREETS
NEW YORK

October 1st., 1.

Mr. Robert Garrett
.36 Continental Building
Baltimore, Md.

Dear Mr. Garrett:

By my hands have you the ar bulletin i
a gold dollar of 1856 with a trifle larger let-
ering on obverse and reverse and the amount
of the years both before and after. There are
apparently two varieties of this year, but
of which we have, and I am tr to a list of
many others there are differ or lettering.

Very sincerely yours,

Curator

Mr. Wayland Wood, Curator,
The American Numismatic Society,
Broadway between 155th and 156th Streets,
New York City.

Dear Sir;

Your letter of October 18th is received.   I beg to say
that my brother, John W. Garrett, owns the collection of coins you have
in mind and is much more familiar with it than I am.   I shall therefore
turn your letter over to him for his attention.   Just now he is out of
the city and is not likely to be here much in the immediate future, but
I hope he may find it possible to give the necessary time to reply to
your inquiry.

                              Yours very truly,

RG/JLO

THE CHOATE MEDAL

ISSUED BY

**THE CENTURY ASSOCIATION AND THE
AMERICAN NUMISMATIC SOCIETY**

HERBERT ADAMS, SCULPTOR

THE JOSEPH HODGES CHOATE
MEMORIAL MEDAL

NUMBER ONE OF A SERIES OF MEDALS COMMEMORATIVE
OF MEN DISTINGUISHED FOR PUBLIC SERVICE

The Century Association, having decided to issue a series of commemorative medals in honor of men who have been especially distinguished for public service, in the arts, in letters and in other notable activities, has appointed a committee with power to act. It is in pursuance of this determination that the first of the proposed medals is now to be issued.

In 1919 an exhibition of medals was held in the gallery of the Century Association where it attracted a great deal of attention to this field of sculpture. For this exhibition The American Numismatic Society loaned a considerable number of plaques and medals from its collection. This exhibition constituted a strong argument in support of the idea that a series of Century Association medals should be undertaken, and that these medals be made available to the members through subscriptions.

It is especially fitting that the first medal of the series should commemorate the public services of so great an American as Joseph Hodges Choate. His singular ability in many fields, his charming personality, and the very great measure of accomplishment which rewarded his efforts, mark him as one of the most gifted men that America has produced. "Patriot, Ambassador, Jurist, Orator," the medal rightly proclaims him.

The design of the medal was entrusted to Mr. Herbert Adams, one of our most distinguished sculptors, President of the National Academy of Design, 1917 to 1919, member of the Commission of Fine Arts and a personal friend of Mr. Choate. Mr. Adams' work for the Library of Congress in Washington, St. Bartholomew's Church in New York, the Bryant Statue in Bryant Park, and many statues and memorials throughout the country testify to his eminence as a sculptor. The medal which he has designed is a work of remarkable artistic quality and a very beautiful presentation of the personality of Mr. Choate.

The Committee of the Century Association desires to extend the privilege of subscribing for this medal to other societies of which Mr. Choate was an honored member. Invitations to subscribe were extended to and accepted by the Bar Association, and the Harvard Club, and the privilege of subscribing will be further extended to a limited list of collectors, amateurs and friends of Mr. Choate.

The Committee of the Century Association has been glad to avail itself of the kind cooperation of The American Numismatic Society in publishing the medal and takes this opportunity to express its cordial appreciation of its helpfulness, and has authorized The American Numismatic Society to issue this circular and to accept subscriptions for the medals.

CASS GILBERT, *Chairman* HENRY DE FOREST BALDWIN,
GEORGE F. KUNZ,   AUGUSTUS TACK,
EDWIN H. BLASHFIELD,

    Committee on Medals of the Century Association.

The Committee on the Publication of Medals of The American Numismatic Society has accepted the invitation of the Century Association to cooperate in publication of the Choate Medal, and has much pleasure in inviting subscriptions for the medal from its members, from the members of the Century Association, from the Bar Association, the Harvard Club, and from a limited list of collectors, amateurs and friends of Mr. Choate.

The medal is an unusually beautiful example of medallic art and will be much prized by its possessors on account of its historical importance, its subject, and its very exceptional artistic merit.

Copies of the medal will be issued in silver and bronze. The price of the medal in SILVER is $10.00, and that of the BRONZE medal, $5.00.

Subscriptions stating the number desired in each metal, accompanied by checks to the order of The American Numismatic Society, should be addressed to The American Numismatic Society, Broadway and 156th Street, New York City.

W. GEDNEY BEATTY, *Chairman,* ROBERT J. EIDLITZ,
WILLIAM B. OSGOOD FIELD, SYDNEY P. NOE,

Committee on the Publication of Medals, The American Numismatic Society.

February 14, 1922.

American Numismatics Society,
156 Street near Broadway,
New York, N. Y.

Dear Sirs:-

   I enclose my check to your
order for $5.75 and shall be much obliged
if you will send me a copy of the descrip-
tive catalog of Greek coins selected from
the collection of Mr. Clarence S. Bement
by T. L. Comparette.

     Very truly yours,

JEG/S

DEKADRACHM OF SYRACUSE
Issued for the Assinarian Games

Descriptive Catalogue of Greek Coins Selected from the Collection of Mr. Clarence S. Bement, of Philadelphia

, 1922

By T. L. COMPARETTE, Curator of the Numismatic Collection, the Mint at Philadelphia. 4to, (about) 100 pages and 25 plates. Price, $3.75 (actual cost). In press and ready soon.

This catalogue embraces 370 of the rarer and more interesting coins in Mr. Bement's splendid collection. It is not a mere catalogue that would be of service only to the expert, but has been compiled with copious notes relating to the cities and states that issued the coins, also to art and artists, literature, history, commerce, finance, and religious matters, that will help the layman to understand the types and the significance of the weights and other facts about ancient coins. The specimens described represent almost the entire Greek world and extend from the early sixth down to the first century B. C. All of the coins are illustrated.

The edition will be small and orders for copies will be entered in the order received until the edition is exhausted.

Aes Signatum

By the same Author. 4to, 61 pages and 6 plates. Price, $1.25. 1919.

A searching study of the great bars that many scholars have accepted as specimens of the first coins issued by the Romans, the aes signatum mentioned by Pliny. Former theories are stated and refuted, and a new explanation of the bars advanced, supported by exhaustive discussions of the types of six bars. Only a few copies left.

"Debasement" of the Silver Coinage Under the Emperor Nero

By the same Author. 4to, 13 pages. Price, $0.35.

The introduction of a sound financial principle into the Roman monetary system. Very few copies left.

The last two works are separate prints from the American Journal of Numismatics.

Orders may be sent to MR. CLARENCE S. BEMENT, 3907 Spruce Street, Philadelphia, Pa., or to THE AMERICAN NUMISMATIC SOCIETY, 156th Street, near Broadway, New York City.

THE AMERICAN NUMISMATIC SOCIETY
BROADWAY, BETWEEN 155TH
AND 156TH STREETS
NEW YORK

March 7th, 1922

John W. Garrett, Esq.
    Garrett Building
        Baltimore, Md.

Dear Mr. Garrett:

    I am enclosing a list of books, and

I note that Lot 202 is Lane-Poole's Mo-

hammedan Dynasties which you wanted.

        Very truly yours,

                                Curator

HW/E
Enc.

March 8, 1922.

Dear Mr. Wood:-

Many thanks for your letter of
March 7th and your reference to Lane-Poole's
"Mohammadan Dynasties" which I have ordered.

Yours very sincerely,

Mr. Howland Wood,
American Numismatic Society,
Broadway & 156th St.,
New York, N. Y.

March 14, 1922.

Dear Mr. Wood:-

My brother has recently given me
a letter you wrote him on the 18th of October,
asking whether a gold dollar of 1858 in my collection was of the rare type with larger letter
ing on the obverse and reverse.   I regret to
say that the only 1858 gold dollar I have is of
the common or ordinary variety.

I do not know when I shall be
in New York again and I am wondering perhaps
when you get through with your very kind
identification of the Mohammadan coins I left
with you, if you will be good enough to send
them to me here in Baltimore.

Very truly yours,

Mr. Howland Wood, Curator,
The American Numismatic Society,
Broadway near 155th St.,
New York, N. Y.

THE AMERICAN NUMISMATIC SOCIETY
BROADWAY, BETWEEN 155TH
AND 156TH STREETS
NEW YORK

March 10th, 1922

John W. Garrett, Esq.
Redwood Street, Corner South
Baltimore, Md.

Dear Mr. Garrett:

I have been so busy with a number of rush
things that I have not gotten around to identifying your Mohammedan coins, but I have them
in plain sight as a reminder and will fix them
up for you as soon as I can.

As near as I can make out, we have got
about the only specimen of that 1858 gold dollar.

Very truly yours,

Curator

HW/C

May 19, 1922.

Mr. Howland Wood, Curator,
The American Numismatic Society,
Broadway, between 155th and 156th Sts.,
New York, N. Y.

Dear Mr. Wood:-

I am deeply indebted to you
for the trouble you have taken in regard to
the coins which I left with you some time ago,
and especially appreciative of it in view of
the fact, which I am very sorry to learn, that
you were under the weather.   I hope your
vacation will put you back again in perfectly
good shape.

I am very much interested in the
list of coins you sent me and I look forward
with the greatest pleasure to seeing them, and
I shall probably keep a good many of them.   I
should be much obliged if you would have them, as
well as my own coins, sent to me at the above
address and let me know what expense you have
been put to in the matter.

Very truly yours,

JWG/S

June 6, 1922.

Mr. Howland Wood, Curator,
American Numismatic Society,
Broadway, between 155th and 156th Sts.,
New York, N. Y.

Dear Mr. Wood:-

I have now been able to go over the
coins you were good enough to send me and have decided
to take nearly all of them.   I am returning one gold
and twenty-two silver pieces, and enclose my check to
your order for the remainder.   I am greatly obliged
to you for giving me this opportunity to add some very
desirable pieces to my collection.

I want to thank you once more for your
kindness and the trouble you have given yourself in
going over the coins from my collection that I left
at the Numismatic Society some time ago.

With best wishes for your vacation,
I am,

Sincerely yours,

JWG/S

OFFICE OF
THE SECRETARY

TELEPHONE
AUDUBON 2484

CABLE ADDRESS
"NUMISMA" NEW YORK

MUSEUM OPEN
10 - 5. WEEK-DAYS
1 - 5. SUNDAYS

LIBRARY OPEN
10 - 5. WEEK-DAYS

THE AMERICAN NUMISMATIC SOCIETY
BROADWAY. BETWEEN 155TH
AND 156TH STREETS
NEW YORK

June 7th, 1922

John W. Garrett, Esq.
    Redwood Street
        Baltimore, Md.

Dear Mr. Garrett:

    In Mr. Wood's absence, I take pleasure in
replying to your letter of June 6th addressed
to him, enclosing your cheque for $232.15 to
cover cost of the gold and silver coins forwarded to you for selection.   Thank you very much
for this, and I am glad that you found so many
desirable pieces to add to your collection.

    The owner of this collection of coins is
General V. Starosselsky, now a resident of California.

                    Very truly yours,

                    Sydney P. Noe

                            Secretary

SPN/E

        P.S. The package containing the coins
              returned by you has come safely to
              hand, for which I thank you.

FREDERICK HOTELS.
LIMITED.

HOTEL GREAT CENTRAL, LONDON
HOTEL RUSSELL, LONDON.
HOTEL MAJESTIC, HARROGATE.
ROYAL PAVILION HOTEL, FOLKESTONE.
HOTEL BURLINGTON, DOVER.
GRANVILLE HOTEL, BEXHILL ON SEA.
HOTEL METROPOLE, WHITBY.
HOTEL BRISTOL, BEAULIEU-SUR-MER.

TELS. HOTEL RUSSELL, LONDON.
TEL. MUSEUM, 1000/S-1720/3.
PRIVATE BRANCH EXCHANGE.

Hôtel Russell.
Russell Square.
London. W.C.1.

July 30 1922

My dear Mr. Garrett

I am finding a few interesting pieces for you most of which will be sent me in September. I bought from a private collector here his work quite a fine old stater of Diodotus which I will send you by registered mail to-morrow. May send a few other pieces later

Sydney P. Noe

THE FREDERICK HOTELS,
LIMITED.

HOTEL GREAT CENTRAL, LONDON.
HOTEL RUSSELL, LONDON.
HOTEL MAJESTIC, HARROGATE.
ROYAL PAVILION HOTEL, FOLKESTONE.
HOTEL BURLINGTON, DOVER.
SACKVILLE HOTEL, BEXHILL ON SEA.
HOTEL METROPOLE, WHITBY.
HOTEL BRISTOL, BEAULIEU-SUR-MER.

Hôtel Russell,
Russell Square,
London, W.C.1

TELEGRAMS, HOTEL RUSSELL, LONDON,
TELEPHONE, MUSEUM, 1000/5-1720/3,
(PRIVATE BRANCH EXCHANGE)

2

19

As I do not like to carry
them around with me.
The price of the gold piece
is #300 (very reasonable)
and if you decide to keep
it will you please
remit to Madison Ave
Branch, Guaranty Trust
Co. for my credit, 60th
St. + Madison Ave. N.Y.C.
With best regards
Yours very truly
Wayte Raymond

Aug 12 1922

Dear Mr Garrett:—

In today's mail
I received from Mr. Wayte Raymond, a gold stater of Diodotus
which he has asked me to forward
to you. If you are still in Bar
Harbor and wish it forwarded,
I shall be happy to send it —
it seemed wise to ask whether
you desired this before sending
the piece through the mail.

With cordial regards,

Yours very sincerely
Sydney P —

OFFICE OF
THE SECRETARY

TELEPHONE
AUDUBON 2484

CABLE ADDRESS
"NUMISMA" NEW YORK

MUSEUM OPEN
10 - 5. WEEK-DAYS
1 - 5. SUNDAYS

LIBRARY OPEN
10 - 5. WEEK-DAYS

THE AMERICAN NUMISMATIC SOCIETY
BROADWAY. BETWEEN 155TH
AND 156TH STREETS
NEW YORK

August 1st, 1922.

Mr. John W. Garrett,
Baltimore,
Maryland.

Dear Sir:-

Herewith is a list of duplicate books
from the library of The American Numismatic Society.
The length of the list is due to our having come into
possession of a considerable library during the past
year. The prices quoted are net, and do not include
carriage. If you can use any of these titles kindly
send me word at once because orders will be filled as
soon as received and preference will therefore lie
with those who order first.

Very truly yours,

Secretary and Librarian.

August 19, 1922.

Mr. Sydney P. Noe,
c/o American Numismatic Society,
156th St., west of Broadway,
New York, N. Y.

Dear Mr. Noe:-

          I am engaged in a political contest
at the moment which is absorbing my entire time and
I am obliged to postpone even consideration of any
other matters.   Your note to me has been forwarded
from Bar Harbor where I have not been able to be at
all this summer.   I am sorry I cannot take up Mr
Raymond's offer at the present time, but I hope I
may be able to do so in the Fall.   Thank you for
writing me and I should be very grateful if you are
having any correspondence with Mr. Raymond, if you
would convey this information to him.

                    Very truly yours,

J.G/S

THE AMERICAN NUMISMATIC SOCIETY
BROADWAY BETWEEN 155TH
AND 156TH STREETS
NEW YORK

10/17/22.

BAMBOO MONEY

In a letter to John Robinson, Salem, Mass., dated
Aug. 11, 1912, Henry Ramsden mentions the "bamboo talley
money". "Their having values written on them, as well
as the names of the issuers and other legends similar to
regular coinage, gives them an interest which the
ordinary bamboo tallies, used for counting or checking
purposes, have not got".

"I find very little has ever been said about them".

Under date of Jan. 8th, 1912, he says of a piece
submitted, "this was perhaps more of a talley than
actual money, as may perhaps turn out to be the case
with all these bamboo pieces, although perhaps, like many
other counters and tokens, may at some time or other
passed as currency".

In an advertisement in the Numismatic and Philatelic
Journal of Japan, for April 1913, Henry Ramsden states
that the bamboo money "is supposed to have been derived
from metal checks said to have been current in the city
of Tsi-an-fu, the capital of Shantung, as far back as
A. D. 1275........ These bamboo pieces are now found in

Bamboo Money

nearly all parts of China, although they appear
to be most popular on the Yangtse and conter-
minous regions.

Their field of circulation was, as a rule,
purely local, although no few extended over the
limits to which they were first intended.......".

December 15, 1922.

Mr. Howland Wood, Curator,
American Numismatic Society,
Broadway at 156th St.,
New York, N. Y.

Dear Mr. Wood:-

I enclose my check to the
order of the Society for the Mohammedan
coins which I bought the other day.

I want to thank you once more
for the help you have been to me in regard
to them and other matters.   After you have
had time to "dope" out the few pieces I left
with you, would you mind sending them to me
here.

Best wishes for a Merry
Christmas and Happy New Year.

Sincerely yours,

JWG/S

December 15, 1922.

Mr. John Reilly,
c/o American Numismatic Society,
Broadway at 156th St.,
New York, N. Y.

Dear Mr. Reilly:-

I am enclosing rubbings of three
Chinese dollars in my collection and one small gold
Rebel piece, and I wonder whether it would be too
much trouble to write under them the names of the
presidents whose protraits they bear, and send them
back to me.

       Merry Christmas.

         Sincerely yours,

JWG/S

OFFICE OF
THE CURATOR

TELEPHONE
AUDUBON 2484

CABLE ADDRESS
"NUMISMA" NEW YORK

MUSEUM OPEN
10 - 5. WEEK-DAYS
1 - 5. SUNDAYS

LIBRARY OPEN
10 - 5. WEEK-DAYS

THE AMERICAN NUMISMATIC SOCIETY
BROADWAY, BETWEEN 155TH
AND 156TH STREETS
NEW YORK

December 16th, 1922.

John W. Garrett, Esq.,
    Garrett Building,
        Baltimore, Md..

Dear Mr. Garrett:-

    Many thanks for your cheque, and I trust
that you will find plenty to do on coins until I
see you again. I forgot to ask you whether you
wanted the British Museum Catalogue on Persian
Coins. We have a duplicate here for sale.

    Wishing you the compliments of the
season,- I am,

                Yours very truly,

                                    Curator.

THE AMERICAN NUMISMATIC SOCIETY
BROADWAY, BETWEEN 155TH AND 156TH STREETS
NEW YORK

December 19th, 1922.

Mr. John W. Garrett,
    Garrett Building,
        Baltimore, Md.

Dear Sir:-

As we desire to make our records as complete as possible, we are sending you the enclosed card which we would be very glad to have you fill out and return to us. This will keep us in a little closer touch with our members, and we can therefore render better service by knowing just what interests them.

Yours very truly,

Acting Secretary.

MUSEUM OPEN
10 - 5. WEEK-DAYS
1 - 5. SUNDAYS

LIBRARY OPEN
10 - 5. WEEK-DAYS

THE AMERICAN NUMISMATIC SOCIETY
BROADWAY, BETWEEN 155TH
AND 156TH STREETS
NEW YORK

December 19th 1922.

Dear Mr Garrett: —

I am delighted to have your note
and the enclosed rubbings.

The gold piece was issued by the Yünänfu
mint by T'ang Chi-yao, the "Tuchün" of
Yünän province, and bears his portrait.

Obv. — Over the head," T'ang, Governor General
(of the) Military Government."

Rev. — " Gold Coin Commemorating the Defence of the
Republic" and, below the stars," Equivalent
to Five Silver Dollars". The flags are those
of the Republic.

Mr A. M. Tracey Woodward has given the history
of this issue in the New China Review for
June 1921.   T'ang also produced two types
of silver half dollars, a bronze fifty cash and
a ten dollar gold piece.

Your next one is, of course, the same. This
one is the first republican dollar. Minted
at Nanking in 1912.

December 21st,1922.

Mr. John W. Garrett,
Garrett Bldg.,
Baltimore, Md.

Dear Sir:

The Society's collection of decorations and war medals has so greatly increased during the past two years that the swing-cases for exhibiting it prove entirely inadequate. Unfortunately, one-third of the collection is not on view owing to this lack of space.

The swing-cases are hung on two sides of each of the four columns in the exhibition room, and it has been found practicable, by providing larger bases, to hang five cases instead of the present three to the columns, thereby increasing our exhibition space by two-thirds.

The additional sixteen cases will provide adequate space for this valuable collection, which is probably the largest and most important in existence. The Society feels that it owes to the memory of the late Mr. J. Sanford Saltus, its friend and benefactor, proper provision for the display of the collection in which he took such great interest and to which he contributed the largest part of its treasures.

These new cases, together with the larger bases, will cost approximately $1,000. Two of the Society's members have already contributed $100. each. It would be greatly appreciated if you could see your way clear to assist in the matter of raising the necessary amount for this purpose.

Trusting you will lend your support, and that we may receive a cheque from you made out to the order of The American Numismatic Society, I am,

December 21, 1922.

Mr. Rowland Wood, Curator,
American Numismatic Society,
Broadway at 156th St.,
New York, N. Y.

Dear Mr. Wood:-

I think I should like to have the British
Museum catalog on Persian coins which you mention in your
letter of December 16th if it does not cost very much.

I have been going over the Mohammedan coins
and find there are lots of "holes" in my collection, which
I hope you may be able perhaps to help me fill up.

In regard to the card which I return herewith,
I might add that my collection, or rather the collection
made by my father and to which my brother and I have added,
consists of a pretty complete series of our Colonial and
Continental coins, including a number of great rarity; a
very complete series of American Mint issues; nearly 400
Patterns of the Philadelphia Mint; a good series of Hard-time
Tokens; "Confederate" pieces; and hundreds of medals, including
some of the rare Presidential ones.   I am not adding to the
above series at present.   Something over one-half of the
California and other private issues are also represented in the
collection, half of the pieces there being unique so far as
I know.   some

- I have not yet begun really to specialize,
although I think I am tending that way.   Aside from the
Greek series which interest me at present, most of all, I
have been, as you know, interest in the Mohammedan coins
and in European issues before 1500.   I have also a pretty
good series of Byzantine gold and a number of Imperial
Roman Aurei.   There is also a number of Confederate,
Broken-bank and Fractional notes, but I have not yet even
checked them up.

If you want more details I shall be only too glad
to give them to you.   Again with best Complements of the
Season.

Sincerely yours,

J.G:S

December 21, 1922.

Mr. John Reilly, Jr.,
c/o American Numismatic Society,
Broadway at 156 th Sts,
New York, N. Y.

Dear Mr. Reilly:-

Many thanks for your answer
to my letter and the interesting information
you give me.

Again with best wishes,

Sincerely yours,

JWG/S

OFFICE OF
THE SECRETARY

TELEPHONE
AUDUBON 2484

CABLE ADDRESS
"NUMISMA" NEW YORK

MUSEUM OPEN
10 - 5. WEEK-DAYS
1 - 5. SUNDAYS

LIBRARY OPEN
10 - 5. WEEK-DAYS

THE AMERICAN NUMISMATIC SOCIETY
BROADWAY. BETWEEN 155TH
AND 156TH STREETS
NEW YORK

December 26th, 1922

John W. Garrett, Esq.
Renwood Street, corner South
Baltimore, Md.

Dear Mr. Garrett:

I am, herewith, returning the coins you left
with me.

The imitation Venetian ducat and the French
Feudal coin, I was unable to locate.

The British Museum Catalogue of Persian coins
is listed at £1.5.0; you can have this for $5.00.
We also have a two-volume catalogue of Byzantine
coins of the B.M. This is listed at £2.5.0. As
the cover of one of the volumes is water-stained and
a little bruised, you can have the two books for Ten
Dollars.

Trusting to see you soon, and with best wishes
for the Coming Year, I am

Very truly yours,

Curator

HW/E
Encs.

January 2, 1923.

Mr. Howland Wood, Curator,
American Numismatic Society,
Broadway at 156th St.,
New York, N. Y.

Dear Mr. Wood:-

Thanks very much for the coins
you returned and for your identification of them
as far as possible.   I should like to have the
British Museum catalog of Persian coins, but I
have the B.M. catalog of Byzantine coins already.

With best wishes for the New Year,

Sincerely yours,

JWG/S

January 2, 1922.

Mr. Edward T. Newell, President,
American Numismatic Society,
Broadway at 156th St.,
New York, N. Y.

Dear Sir:-

I shall be glad to contribute $50.00,
for which I enclose my check, toward the object
mentioned in your letter of December 21st.   I
am sorry that I cannot be present at the meeting
of the Council on January 12th, but I shall not
be able to leave Baltimore at that time.

        With best wishes for the New Year,

            Sincerely yours,

JWG:S

OFFICE OF
THE PRESIDENT

TELEPHONE
AUDUBON 2484

MUSEUM OPEN
10 · 5. WEEK-DAYS
1 · 5. SUNDAYS

LIBRARY OPEN
10 · 5. WEEK-DAYS

11

THE AMERICAN NUMISMATIC SOCIETY
BROADWAY. BETWEEN 155TH
AND 156TH STREETS
NEW YORK

January 4th, 1923.

John W. Garrett, Esq.,
    Garrett Building,
        Baltimore, Md.

Dear Mr. Garrett:-

On behalf of The American Numismatic
Society, I desire to thank you most sincerely
for your generous gift toward the cost of the
swing cases we are providing for our decorations
and war medals.

Very truly yours,

Edward T. Newell

President.

THE AMERICAN NUMISMATIC SOCIETY
BROADWAY, BETWEEN 155TH
AND 156TH STREETS
NEW YORK

January 6th, 1913

John W. Garrett, Esq.
Garrett Building
Baltimore, Md.

Dear Mr. Garrett:

I have had sent to you today the
copy of the British Museum Catalogue
of Persian coins, as you requested, and
trust same will reach you with no delay.

Very truly yours,

Director

January 8, 1923.

Mr. Howland Wood, Curator,
American Numismatic Society,
Broadway at 156th St.,
New York, N. Y.

De r Mr. Wood:-

Thanks very much for the
catalog of Persian coins today received
and for which I send you my check for
$5.00.   I hope to be in New York towards
the end of the month and to have the chance
of seeing you ag_in then.

Sincerely yours,

J.G/S

THE AMERICAN NUMISMATIC SOCIETY
BROADWAY, BETWEEN 155TH
AND 156TH STREETS
NEW YORK

January 7 , 1908

J. W. Garrett, Esq.
Garrett Building
Baltimore, Md.

Dear Mr. Garrett:

I beg to acknowledge receipt of your cheque
for Five Dollars (\$5.00) to cover cost of the
book on Persian coins.   Thank you very.

I am sending you, under separate cover, a
book catalogue from Paul Gauthier. Although this
particular number has comparatively little of numismatics in it, I thought that perhaps if you
did not know of it to be sent, you might be interested.

Very truly yours,

OFFICE OF
THE PRESIDENT

TELEPHONE
AUDUBON 2484

MUSEUM OPEN
10 - 5, WEEK-DAYS
1 - 5, SUNDAYS
LIBRARY OPEN
10 - 5, WEEK-DAYS

THE AMERICAN NUMISMATIC SOCIETY
BROADWAY, BETWEEN 155TH
AND 156TH STREETS
NEW YORK

January 25th, 1923

John A. Garrett, Esq.
Garrett Building
Baltimore, Md.

Dear Mr. Garrett:

It would give me much pleasure to have
you serve on the Oriental Coins Committee,
of which Mr. Wood is Chairman, during the
term of 1923.

Trusting this may be agreeable to you,

Very sincerely yours,

Edward T. Newell

President

Mr. Howland Wood, Curator,
American Numismatic Society,
Broadway at 156th St.,
New York, N. Y.

Dear Mr. Wood:-

Please forgive me if I seem to bombard
you with letters, but I lean upon you for advice.

I am sending you today three coins.
One of them I have just received from Schulman, who
classes it as a Guadaloupe piece.   You will see that
it has a number of countermarks on it and I am sure
you will be able to tell me what they all mean.   I
shall be very grateful if you will.   The other two
pieces are Chinese Sycee and have also been sent me
by Schulman.   I wonder if Riley could compare these
with the pieces Schulman recently sent him.   As I
remember the latter these do not seem to be as good.
Riley was going to let me know if he did not want any of
the ones Schulman had sent him, so that I might pick out
one or two of them for my own collection.   Schulman
asks 35 and 15 florins for the two pieces he has sent
me.   I should like to know how they compare with the
other lot if it is not asking too much of Riley and
yourself.

                    Sincerely yours,

JWG/S

OFFICE OF
THE SECRETARY

TELEPHONE
AUDUBON 2484

CABLE ADDRESS
"NUMISMA" NEW YORK

MUSEUM OPEN
10 - 5. WEEK-DAYS
1 - 5 SUNDAYS

LIBRARY OPEN
10 - 5. WEEK DAYS

THE AMERICAN NUMISMATIC SOCIETY
BROADWAY, BETWEEN 155TH
AND 156TH STREETS
NEW YORK

J......., ...t , ...

John W. Garrett, Esq.
Roland Street
Baltimore, Md.

Dear Mr. Garrett:

Please pardon the delay in replying to your letter of Ja. 9th, but for the past few days I have been attending our Annual Meeting.

Your gold coin is a nice piece; and if you can get it at a reasonable, I would advise you to take it, as such coins are disappearing and are now becoming decidedly scarce. Unfortunately I cannot assign it to any one locality. I should say that it was used on one of the French, rather than on one of the English, as the English system of weights was different, and nearly all the pieces used on their island had gold plugs inserted to bring the weight to their standard. This piece was probably used at loupe although I have no means of identifying it.

From my study of these pieces, I have come to the conclusion that many of the were issued more or less privately, as these were or of the people and not issued by the Island Governments to be used as the gold coins in use on these Islands.

This identical piece is Lot ...11 in the Dr. J. ...son ...lli Collection, sold by ...lman, ... 23rd, 1910. In the description of lot, he notes "L. for Guadeloupe B. for ...; M. for Martinical L. for Los Saintes, but personally I do not consider these as locality marks, but assessment marks.

The two Chinese pieces are quite similar to those at Reilly, though the inscriptions are a little different. Of these, there were several sold...

one of ... of 15 florins. Reilly says that he is going to reply soon, and that you can deduct as ... ... sent to him.

Sincerely ...

January 25, 1923.

Mr. Howland Wood, Curator,
American Numismatic Society,
Broadway at 156th St.,
New York, N. Y.

Dear Mr. Wood:-

Thanks very much for your
letter of the 17th and for the trouble you
have taken about my request regarding certain
coins that I have now received back from you.

Very sincerely yours,

JWG/S

P.S.   Thanks very much for the book catalog
from Paul Ceuthner which you were good enough
to send me.

January 15, 1923.

Mr. Edward T. Newell, President.
American Numismatic Society.
Broadway at 156th St.,
New York, N. Y.

Dear Mr. Newell:-

      I should be very glad
to serve on the Oriental Coin Committee,
of which Mr. Wood is Chairman, during the
term of 1923.

      Very sincerely yours,

JAG/S

Metropolitan Museum of Art,

New York.

Dear Sirs:-

I have recently come into possession of a
collection of some 4000 Medieval European coins,
particularly rich in so far as concerns the Medieval
coins of Germany. Inasmuch as my speciality is
directed towards Russian coins - od which I have the
finest collection outside of Russia - I am interested
in disposing of my Medieval coins.

At the present time foreign buyers are
negotiating with me for the sale of these coins bur
as an American I should prefer to see them transferred to
American hands.

I would, therefore, be very pleased to hear
from you as to whether you would be interested in the
purchase of the collection.

Very sincerely,

(signed) J. Rives Childs

American Express Co.
Berlin.

THE AMERICAN NUMISMATIC SOCIETY
BROADWAY, BETWEEN 155TH
AND 156TH STREETS
NEW YORK

February 6th, 1923

John J. Garrett, Esq.
Garrett Building
Baltimore, Md.

Dear Mr. Garrett:

We received the enclosed letter from
J. Rives Childs, and it occurs to me that
you may be interested to follow it up. If
not, would you be so good as to return the
letter to us at your convenience.

Very truly yours,

Curator

Hoyt
Enc.

February 9, 1923.

Mr. Howland Wood, Curator,
American Numismatic Society,
Broadway at 156th St.,
New York, N. Y.

Dear Mr. Wood:-

I am much obliged to you for sending me Mr. J.
Rives Childs' letter which I return herewith as you
request.   Whether I should be interested or not is
difficult for me to say.   The buying of a whole
collection does not appeal to me very much because it
takes away the fun of collecting; and I am particularly
not interested in German coins.   If there were a
good series of French or Italian Mediaeval coins I
might be interested, but I would, of course, have to
know all the necessary details including the price
asked, and I would have to figure on that quite care-
fully before I could make up my mind.   I might find it
possible to go in for certain parts of such a collection
together with the Society or other interested purchasers.

Very truly yours,

JWG/S

Encl

OFFICE OF
THE SECRETARY

TELEPHONE
AUDUBON 2484

CABLE ADDRESS
"NUMISMA" NEW YORK

MUSEUM OPEN
10 - 5, WEEK-DAYS
1 - 5, SUNDAYS

LIBRARY OPEN
10 - 5, WEEK-DAYS

THE AMERICAN NUMISMATIC SOCIETY
BROADWAY, BETWEEN 155TH
AND 156TH STREETS
NEW YORK

February 10th, 1913

John W. Garrett, Esq.
Garrett Building
Baltimore, Md.

Dear Mr. Garrett:

I think the Museum would not attempt to
negotiate for the collection of Mediaeval
European coins, and I am sending Mr. Gillas' letter to another collector.

I am enclosing a gold Dinar which I show-
ed you some time ago. This you can have for
Five Dollars. If I find out more about it,
I will let you know.

Trusting to see you soon, I am

Very truly yours,

Howland Wood

Curator

Hw/S

March 24th, 1923

Dear Mr. Garrett:

There has been offered to our Society a most
unusual collection of twenty-one Indian Peace Medals.
We have been able to secure an option for Two Thousand
Dollars, expiring on April 1st.

This collection would go far toward completing
the Society's series which already is the finest ex-
tant. The new collection contains several specimens
heretofore quite unknown.

No branch of numismatics should possess a greater
appeal to the _American_ Numismatic Society than the
medals owned, worn and treasured by the first Ameri-
cans - the American Indian.

These medals are rapidly becoming more difficult
to obtain, and the demand for them on the part of collectors and museums is increasing with even greater
rapidity.

At the present moment the Society has no funds
available in which to take advantage of such an unusual
opportunity. Will you not send in a contribution?

Very truly yours,

Edward T. Newell

President

John W. Garrett, Esq.
Baltimore, Md.

March 27, 1923.

Mr. E. T. Newell, President,
American Numismatic Society,
Broadway at 156th St.,
New York, N. Y.

Dear Mr. Newell:-

As you know, I have recently made quite a
large investment in coins, so large indeed, that
at least until I am able to dispose of those that
are duplicates of pieces already in my collection,
I do not feel able to make any further outlay on
coins.

I appreciate the wonderful chance that is
offered to the Society in connection with the
twenty-one Indian Peace Medals and I wish I could
help you out substantially in raising the $2000.00
necessary, but the best I feel able to do is to send
you my check for $25.00.

With best wishes,

Sincerely yours,

JMG/S
Encl.

OFFICE OF
THE SECRETARY

TELEPHONE
AUDUBON 2484

CABLE ADDRESS
NUMISMA" NEW YORK

THE AMERICAN NUMISMATIC SOCIETY
BROADWAY, BETWEEN 155TH
AND 156TH STREETS
NEW YORK

March 28th, 1923

John W. Garrett, Esq.
Redwood Street, corner South
Baltimore, Md.

Dear Mr. Garrett:

I am enclosing a copy of a catalogue of
Renaissance medals which I think may interest
you.

Mr. A. F. Davies writes us that he has
received instructions to dispose of this collection. He states that an expert has recently examined the medals and discovered but 18
doubtful pieces. He also states that 85 per
cent are absolutely authentic. They are held
at Ten Thousand Dollars ($10,000). The collec-
tion can be seen at 60 Avenue du Bois de Boulogne,
Paris, by appointment with Mr. H. Lowenfeld.

The address of Mr. A. F. Davies is: 134, Sin-
clair Road, West Kensington, London, W.

Very truly yours,

Acting Secretary & Curator

HW/E
Enc.

THE AMERICAN NUMISMATIC SOCIETY
BROADWAY, BETWEEN 155TH
AND 156TH STREETS
NEW YORK

August 9th, 1923

returned with many thanks
(only ?)

John W. Garrett, Esq.
    Seal Harbor, Maine

Dear Mr. Garrett:

    Your letter just at hand, and I have this day
forwarded to you Reinach's histoire, parcel post,
insured.   There is no hurry about returning it.

    I had hoped to see you before you left for the
summer. I trust that you will be able to pay us a
visit on your way back.

    For some months I have been holding $2.50 on
my desk, hoping to give it you the next time you
called here.   It is for an overcharge on those cop-
per Parthian coins and I am now enclosing cheque for
same.

                        Very truly yours,

                        Howland Wood
                                Curator

HW/E

BROADWAY AT 156th STREET
NEW YORK

December 10th, 1923.

Sir:

On behalf of The American Numismatic Society, I beg to acknowledge receipt of your recent generous gift, and to express our hearty appreciation of the interest in the growth of our collection you have thus evidenced.

I am

Yours respectfully,

Acting President.

John W. Garrett, Esq.,
Garrett Building,
Baltimore, Md.

www.ingramcontent.com/pod-product-compliance
Lightning Source LLC
Chambersburg PA
CBHW020555270326
41927CB00006B/856